T0164260

EXIT THEATER

THE COLORADO PRIZE FOR POETRY

EXIT THEATER

MIKE LALA

The Center for Literary Publishing
Colorado State University

For information about permission to reproduce
selections from this book, write to
The Center for Literary Publishing
attn: Permissions
9105 Campus Delivery
Colorado State University
Fort Collins, Colorado 80523-9105.

Printed in the United States of America.

Library of Congress Cataloging-in-Publication Data

Names: Lala, Mike, 1987- author.
Title: Exit theater / Mike Lala.
Description: Fort Collins, Colorado : Colorado State University, The Center
    for Literary Publishing, [2016]. | "The Colorado Prize for Poetry"
Identifiers: LCCN 2016032629 (print) | LCCN 2016035034 (ebook) | ISBN
    9781885635532 (pbk. : alk. paper) | ISBN 9781885635549 (electronic)
Subjects: LCSH: Consumption (Economics)--Moral and ethical aspects--Poetry. |
    Justice--Poetry. | LCGFT: War poetry.
Classification: LCC PS3612.A5428 A6 2016 (print) | LCC PS3612.A5428 (ebook) |
    DDC 811/.6--dc23
LC record available at https://lccn.loc.gov/2016032629

The paper used in this book meets the minimum requirements of the
American National Standard for Information Sciences-Permanence of Paper
for Printed Library Materials, ANSI Z39.48-1984.

1 2 3 4 5   20 19 18 17 16

Contents

EXIT THEATER

Say Goodbye to the Shores (Catullus 101)

Say goodbye, rudder—curtain, seamstress, stitch.
I'm here for this shit ceremony, to pull you from the hem.
Say goodbye, microphone. Try, but do not speak.
Robbed of voice, say nothing. Fail to end this hush.
Since Luck refuses to let you lend me your hand
or feel my grasp, say goodbye, brother, taken
not given. *Now (at least now) these objects of our history*
will pass through us, through history. Say goodbye—
this elegy—*take it, drunk on my salt.* Little mirror,
here's to you: *A drink. The passage. Goodbye.*

SAY   TO THE SHORES

Suite w/ a View for the Ends of Our Days (Three Plinths)

Volta then the five, tall tabletop umbrellas we walked under, down the avenue in alternating shade & sunlight: fake silks, blown glass, bulwark steel edge of sidewalk,[1] taxi cars' yellow aluminum up 6th whispering *Soon* (& finally) *the grain will fail to pollinate*[2]—resource-war combustion engines dimming to a sound *like chirping, tin scraping, electronic voices, & mine, dear, the same, like a phonograph but harsher, variable in both time & pitch, disembodied.* Dusklight w/ you in a room at my fingertips—pink, like it used to be, pink sliding into orange[3] though its arc no longer a constant, perfect gradient, no longer your walking through, walking through. No longer, too, your flush body wraithed in those colors. Only you now, blue, a variant of white. Yes. I catch myself looking through the device:[4] expectation of depth as canary for desire. Two series of surfaces diverge, & by compulsion or habit, being figure & center, I take both.[5] I shoot myself in soft light[6] to make my skin appear smoother. I shoot myself from an angle to be fit.[7] When I sit down & raise my hands to the interface, I forget, for a moment, my genitals. It happens on the blacktop, when it's in my pocket too now, my sex a blurred stream of blue—though less frequently & with more distinguishable measure (& unlike being cut, it makes me feel bodiless); I'd do it on the reg if I could like a yo-yo does kinetics, ambulatory & complete.[8] I like my lips *red*,[9] despite the petroleum,[10] the forests cleared in Indonesia.[11] My legs belong in selvedge,[12] though its dyeing process ends in benzene sodium hy-

[1]Steel-faced curbing began to be installed in New York City at the turn of the 20th century. In keeping with NYC DOT Standard Details of Construction[1.1] and its Instructions for Filing Plans & Guidelines for the Design of Sidewalks, Curbs, Roadways and Other Infrastructure Components,[1.2] this feature of New York's sidewalks has become almost ubiquitous throughout the city, as the guidelines stipulate that any new sidewalk or curbing installed be of equal or greater strength than that pre-existing on the block. It is, to me, a defining feature of my city, noticeable almost anywhere one walks.

[2]Global warming trends will soon (and have already started to) upset the global balance and production of food. "Just like us, our crops are adapted to the Holocene, the 11,000-year period of climatic stability we're now leaving . . . In the course of this month, a quadrillion kernels of corn need to pollinate across the grain belt, something they can't do if temperatures remain off the charts."[2.1 2.2]

[3]Blur.[3.1]

[4]I, more frequently than I'd like to admit, catch myself in a lapse of attention, trying to look through, not at, my phone. Similar effects of the increasing integration of technology into our lives have been well-researched and documented, including loss of memory (radiation),[4.1] and reliance on the cloud for 'everyday' memorization (laziness).[4.2 4.3] It reminds me of the lines . . .

[5]Frost wrote in "The Road Not Taken":[5.1] "Two roads diverged in a wood" and, "sorry [he] could not travel both," "be[ing only] one traveler" he "took the [road] less traveled" – making all the difference. Whatever that means, or meant, I always ask, when I re-read those words now, looking down at my phone, *Why not travel both?*

[6]Snap.[6.1]

[7]Snap.[7.1]

[8]Whirr.[8.1]

3

drosulphite water runoff.[13] I read the paper (online) & a man (Russ George) sprayed a whale's volume of iron dust from his charter in the Pacific.[14] He spurred a growth of plankton visible from orbit[15] &, through that act, his hand extends. Unlike the bees,[16] another round of workers,[17] their garments, the coal, then the fish.[18] Though their images go on, in keeping with dominion's logic—*syntax of bracketed words*[19]—the dream of coexisting, much less with other species, is a dream that has already ended. Now,[20] an arctic bear eats its offspring[21] in the palm of your hand as I recoil. Its footfalls echo down a relay[22] to the open window's repetitions from a spire singeing sparrows who would otherwise be singing *Here they come.*

[1.3] http://www.nyc.gov/html/ddc/downloads/pdf/pub_intra_std/_DOT/hwy_std_constr_details_100701.pdf

[1.4] http://www.nyc.gov/html/dot/downloads/pdf/instfilingplan.pdf

[1.5] http://www.rollingstone.com/politics/news/global-warmings-terrifying-new-math-20120719#ixzz3nQO3WWil

[1.5] http://www.ncbi.nlm.nih.gov/pmc/articles/PMC3761068/

[1.5] http://img12.deviantart.net/b088/i/2011/030/9/8/gradient_purple_pink_orange_by_einstud-d38es5u.jpg

[4.1] https://www.rfsafe.com/loss-memory-link-smartphones-cell-phone-radiation/

[4.3] http://www.scientificamerican.com/article/the-internet-has-become-the-external-hard-drive-for-our-memories/

[4.4] http://www.huffingtonpost.com/2013/12/11/technology-changes-memory_n_4414778.html

[5] http://www.poetryfoundation.org/poem/173536

[6] https://www.dropbox.com/s/zrc4ds0xh5jbg1a/2014-04-23%2019.46.07.jpg?dl=0

[7] https://www.dropbox.com/sc/oz1zx1se3vjiws7/AACZG_KiHngyg3UVcq2aZXxma?oref=e&n=14979599

[8] http://giphy.com/gifs/yoyos-gifmania-Y4IYDRnpXAgFy/fullscreen

[9] https://www.facebook.com/photo.php?fbid=10103476472562934&set=a.10100340576977824.3062842.2337981&type=3&theater

[9] http://www.revlon.com/products/lips/lip-color/revlon-ultra-hd-lipstick?utm_source=google&utm_medium=cpc&utm_term=%2Bbest%20%2Bred%20%2Blipsticks&utm_campaign=Unbranded+Lipstick+-+B&utm_content=suHTTxgZU%7Cdc_pcrid_52789698456#309975564952110

[9.1] http://www.maccosmetics.com/product/13854/310/Products/Makeup/Lips/Lipstick/Lipstick#/shade/Brave_Red

[9.1] http://www.organicmakeup.ca/ca/PetroleumCosmetics.asp

[11] http://www.theguardian.com/environment/2004/mar/07/lifeandhealth.supermarkets

[12] http://3x1.us/shop/men/m3-xx133/

[13] https://www.doria.fi/bitstream/handle/10024/42825/A1388%20Vuorema.pdf

[14] https://en.wikipedia.org/wiki/Russ_George

[15] http://russgeorge.net/wp-content/uploads/2013/03/Vancouver_AMO_2006176_lrg-624x8111.jpg

[16] http://russgeorge.net/wp-content/uploads/2013/03/storymaker-superorganisms-plankton-red-tide-algae8-515x388.jpg

[9] Lipstick is the one makeup product to which I am absolutely—hallelujiah, praise *something*—*not* allergic, and which I enjoy wearing, especially on Halloween. I particularly like a bright cherry or burnished red (cliché, I know), though a good filter on a smartphone can make my lips look pink.[9.1] I am, however, reticent to purchase a stick for myself (seems rather wasteful for such limited use). The generous reader might consider purchasing one for me.[9.2] [9.3] Mail it to Mike Lala, 760 Grand Street Apt. 3L, Brooklyn, NY 11211. I'll be thankful…

[10] …even if you're poisoning me (most lipstick contains petroleum…[10.1]

[11] …and palm oil,[11.1] the harvesting of which is responsible for massive deforestation and other methods of ecological destruction near the equator).

[12] Likewise, my favorite jeans[12.1] (size 32)…

[13] are made with real indigo, which, in the dyeing process, requires setting chemicals that poison water runoff, therefore streams and lakes.[13.1]

[14] Human attempts to mitigate the effects of atmospheric carbon, the undoubted, 100%, I-can't-believe-I'm-even-writing-this cause of climate change, have been proposed at various points by a number of well-intentioned people, some scientists, some sci-fi fans. They argue geoengineering will be a more-effective route (given a narrowing time frame) of carbon mitigation than (not-so-)simply ceasing fossil fuel use. Russ George will, like it or not, probably go down as the first person to attempt a large-scale geoengineering application.[14.1]

[15] …by causing a massive plankton bloom off the western coast of North America (using powderized iron blown from a boat) that was visible from space and capable, if applied on a planetary scale, of processing the carbon built up in the seas.[15.1] [15.2] While climate change has garnered growing attention and concern in recent years…

[16] …perhaps the most eerie of the many effects of human chemical use and dispersion is the unprecedented die-off of bees and other pollinating insects (via neonicotinoids)…[16.1]

[17] …a fact established the same year Bangladeshi factory owners were charged in the fire that killed more than 100 of their workers…[17.1]

[18] …the same year a study found that mercury levels in 84% of all consumable fish are unsafe to eat,[18.1] mercury poisoning being caused by the burning of coal, which enters

[12] http://www.motherjones.com/environment/2015/07/climate-change-killing-bumblebees

[13] http://www.nytimes.com/2013/12/23/world/asia/bangladeshi-factory-owners-charged-in-fatal-fire.html?_r=0

[14] http://www.cbsnews.com/news/study-finds-unsafe-mercury-levels-in-84-percent-of-all-fish/

[15] http://www2.epa.gov/mercury

[16] http://www.theguardian.com/environment/2014/sep/29/earth-lost-50-wildlife-in-40-years-wwf

[17] http://i.dailymail.co.uk/i/pix/2014/02/11/article-0-1B5EA37500000578-587_634x425.jpg

[18] https://www.google.com/search?q=now&oq=now&aqs=chrome..69i57j69i60j69i59j69i60l3.294j0j4&sourceid=chrome&es_sm=91&ie=UTF-8#q=time+now%20%20

[19] http://s1.ibtimes.com/sites/www.ibtimes.com/files/styles/v2_article_large/public/2011/12/09/202426-polar-bear-cannibalism.jpg

[20] https://www.google.com/search?q=cell+phone+relay+towers&espv=2&biw=1339&bih=732&tbm=isch&tbo=u&source=univ&sa=X&ved=0CF8QsARqFQoTCNiGkNSXpMgCFYo6Pgodvwsw&dpr=2

[21], [22] http://www.coldbacon.com/poems/fq.html

the atmosphere (as carbon, mercury, +++) and then permeates the ocean from plant life to bottom feeders up to apex predators, a process known (for any compound) as biomagnification.[18.2]

[19]The incredible level of species extinction currently underway on earth—it's estimated that half of the world's wildlife population has died off since 1970[19.1]—makes me wish for an Ark, a library or archive or at least theoretically collapse-proof DNA depository for every life-form left on earth, though I know the industrial application of that kind of catalog would likely entail more death, more subservience of other forms of life to our own, and would most likely be abused in ways that resemble the National Security Agency's[19.2] work with phone and internet records, for which they are building giant servers in the desert, land that was once plains, and only became desertified after Europeans hunted the bison and other large, land-tilling and fertilizing mammals into extinction . . .

[20]Now,[20.1]

[21]I'd like to end on what I think is *the* image, distilled to a poignancy I will die remembering, of planetary climate change and the legacy of our species, one I would argue gained widespread attention because of *its* species' perceived 'cuteness' and tie to Coca-Cola's holiday advertising campaigns. It's this one,[21.1] of a starving polar bear consuming its offspring, head turned, as if—almost—in shame. I imagine it pacing the ever-shrinking wasteland of its home biosphere, still starving, as . . .

[22]. . . Eliot wrote in "Burnt Norton," "Footfalls echo[ing] in the memory/ Down the passage which we did not take/ Towards the door we never opened." One might, in light of current times, rewrite this phrase as I have. "My words echo/ Thus,[22.1] [on] your [device]."[22.2]

5

[*No photography.*]

Still life with compote and fruit beside
still life with compote, apples, and oranges.

[*No photography.*]

Still life with Purro I beside II. Young sailor
condense the meaning of his body by seeking its essential lines.

[*No photography.*]

Seated nude now not *without* her white scarf
but the scarf no longer hides her pubis.

[*No photography.*]

Goldfish and palette. Interior with goldfish.

Pont Saint-Michel and Police HQ
(the view outside through the window).

[*No photography.*]

Goldfish in bowl atop indistinct surface.
Vase of ivy on chest of drawers.

[*No photography.*]

Laurette as meditation, seated in pink armchair.
Seated in green robe, black background, looking down.

[*No sketching.*] In the light

across the street, three officers
are waiting for her figure to appear.

[*No photography.*]

Notre Dame, night.
Detail, wall. South façade and Seine in daylight

view through window, opposite lamplight
bridge and riverbank overlaid the floorboards, outlined, black.

[*No photography. No drinking.*] [*I'm taking medication.*]

Woman on divan. Woman in an armchair.

Paisley carpet, shuttered windows
variations on the drapes.

[*Stand back, please.*]

Cliff with fish. Cliff with stingrays. Cliff with single eel and white sail.

[*No photography. No sketching. It holds up the crowd.*]

The Large Blue Dress February 26, March 3, March 12
13, 22, 23, 24, 25, April 2 and 3, Dear

Lydia,

Every day, a photograph (I remember—).
Every day, that dress (. . . being stunned).

Every day, blinding in the corner and missing its other half.

[*No photography.*]

Lydia Delectorskaya, the author—
Lydia, the author regrets—

[*No photography.*]

Lydia, the author requests you simply
take your blue dress off.

[*No photography.*]

Point to something. It is not here.
Point because you will die

Lydia,

point as if to say *the bodice
snares your roving eye.*

[*No photography.*] Here

in the last room eight photos one painting
an empty white pedestal in the corner beside me come over here Lydia

and sit on it.

[*Sir—*]

Large red interior. My face in a black fern.

Your hair over me. Interior, twelve people
Egyptian cotton, eight pears, my face, just pictures

the fern outside through the window. Black now.

Light—on a white wall. [*Sir* . . .] Behind us. That year. That war.
[*Sir, stand back please.*] Lydia. You wouldn't believe it, Lydia. All we have

are photographs.

[*Back, please.*]

The Fire that Consumes All before It (Reverse Ilium)

22 years after the Cold War, a stone

on a glass plate, on the second floor
of a rotunda *deuxième tour* a woman

I watch with a woman I love.

    •

Like waters that consume all before them
a man lifts a stone   drops it

on a plate of glass   another

traces the plane of his sight with his hand
points to the sky.

The Korean Peninsula divides.
The first man moves a sea east.

    •

Like a snake that consumes all before it
the woman revolves around a wall.

Like a hawk the woman circles it.
Like a man she pushes forward.

A second man (our third) appears
before the wall.

He stands with his legs apart facing it.

The wall does nothing.

Like a sun the woman revolves behind it.
The war ends. Our first man moves to Paris.

     •

In the country of his birth I bought two
tennis shoes, a jersey with my initials, matching

socks and gym shorts, a backpack
with a cartoon mouse

speaking poor English into a bubble.

I remember the entire stretch of runway
lined with surface missiles pointed north

waking before the city, my mouth open.

     •

Like a mirror that subsumes all before it

the glass beneath the rock casts the shadow
of a rock

breaking glass on the wall behind it.

The 7ᵗʰ Fleet runs exercises off the Sea of Japan.

On the floor of the lobby, there are three
sheets of paper

the woman *like a woman* does not touch.

In the end, these men and women who live
and work in America stand before the wall

and bow.

The man from Korea is not here.   The cellist
I forget to mention   his long black hair

hands   on two bows and the neck
                    of his cello

dissonance gathering forgotten history

he does not bow.

Like a phrase. A fire. A language. A line
there is a wall that does not bow.

A pig before us, it consumes.
A bank what's behind it has vanished.

          ●

A second woman leaps headlong into the arms
of a man   he drops her   a wall falls.

Now, all but the woman
like ashes lie down on the paper and writhe.

Like a fire there is a wall that stands behind them.

Portraits of the Artists as Their Own Subjects

There's a   boring through

the faces on Jonathan's canvases
                    figures (ink and coffee)

opening   black brush strokes.

Above the white cabinets   in his kitchen
generics // two cowboys   horses in taupe

faces / blacked-out // Mary
annulled   beside her   the child

lifting off   its eyes   black brush strokes.

Time came   she hauled her figures
from the water   her children

off the wall   and began (again)

stretching   the women   in her life
in a field   of violet

oiled, bearing teeth   under   each other.

Now she doesn't paint   two jobs
her husband / the hood   of a silver Jaguar

two monks   above him
a desperate   holding down

There's   the grace of a man   on wire

how he swings his legs in an s-curve
over the sidewalk   talking shit

grace of crows' feet   actual birds
of abandonment   sink.   Sink, Matthew

then curve.   It's

hard doing the bidding / of your

tongue / and hand   that intricate devil
leaving his name   on paper

your walk   straight   if you say it.

She moves   from the curtain
          black dress   bare arms

the man   in the pinstriped
          sleeves / her lover

the man with // the chair moves // the man with // no shoes

who makes her be held (*to be in his arms . . .*)
who makes him (*to hold her . . .*) all arms

till he can't
and he drops her
and she turns

to repeat the holding
and repeat being taken
and repeat the falling and turn

as the man in the pinstriped sleeves stands still
in the sound of their breathing   water   on stone

the woman   black dress, bare // arms   flailing
not knowing   should they hold

or what

Wed   and loose some friends
        he leaves them for the home he's built

the band   the friends he's gathered

sing *love*   and   little else.

A chorus and cacophony   behind him   singing *love*

love, love // love, love   *what*

happens   *after love?*

First   the paper   she rolled in
the kitchen   taped down

cooked on, walked over, taped down, torn
smoothed over // over, again.

Then a camera   in the corner
an archive   behind

the portraits / she hung in profile

singing *Dinner's on the table //* then *bones
in the shadowbox //* footprints   on the scroll

from   stove   to sink   and back

She's

running   running backward
running   running backward

running hard   backward
        dear Sarah   say again? Your

                dancers   sweating // breathing
        hard   hey Sarah!

running backward   running

                running backward

Opposite   sawtooth
         horsehair   keeps   ringing

brass   keys   breath   steel.

         You look   so lonely
sitting on an upright trumpet box

fiddling   the valves.

One step / the melody // another / then

down.   *Whose song*   *is it now*
your life   *away—*

F or him   the trash
                 collected due

(he went out at night and turned it)

         brought him home to work
in the darkroom   at the dining table.

In the basement // two images, over-
lapping in the color couplers.

On the table // two structures, working
themselves out.

His elbows / two cities
arms vertical / wrists bent.

Turning   to meet / trying
this height   that

The screen lit up   Old.

She took to foam
      the stitching / cloth   *and it was without form . . .*

Patches   clay   *Ground Theme*
Koji Kondo, 1985 // PVC, green paint, astroturf

      and darkness on the face

of the Kingdom

and her hand over the cellophane water
    her hand over the plush fungi
    her hand over the void
      over the *Pakkun* flower with piranha teeth bare

      and there,

Flags wave   in the dye
cut / up   purple / blue

                                        set out // dry
re-stitched   black.

My America, she—   *dark stars*
          set out / a / part of   what we knew

was blue, deep violet   black.

No red (or white) though   flags still

on the drywall   evening, evening // (on the drywall)

          dark blue

IN THE GUN CABINET

In the gun cabinet, drapery, crushed velvet—*Yes, red*—
    pulled over the fainting couch, the globe stands, the insides of the trumpet cases

the stain, darkened, where my brother cut his finger & drew it into the wood
    the edge of the barrel my father dropped as it pitched & went off

Dusk falls in the gun cabinet
the city in yellow silk

I pull its sash
the first tower

markets, power grids

Mother, take my hand
lead me to the theater's

bold lettering lit
by hydrocarbons

EXIT THEATER

I step in, through the first door
beneath an iron chandelier

my heels click & echo
a regiment, a pattern

past the box office
will call, powder room

side-halls, cocktail lounge
ice trays & ceiling-high mirrors

through the next door
a theater

a needle
weaving carpet

white noise from the speakers, white light
under the curtain

I stand there before it
a face made of gnats

unable to speak
a language I don't

Qu'est-ce que c'est?
it sways—

What is that?
the folds shuffle—

Quid dicis cum nescis quid velis?

Like a parched, Persian-red
tongue strung from the rafters

the curtain hangs mute & still

I step out to the hallways of the gun cabinet to rest
        pick a scallop from the silver, chat the wall-hung former guests

ladle gin from a punch bowl as it calves off an ice floe
        part my hair in a breastplate & plot my way back

making eyes
at the taxidermy

as I exit

There's a violence here

that folds   you
two roads

meet

in the country
under a poplar tree

in the evening

(in the gun cabinet, evening)
over the power lines

slack   a fence missing pickets

the house now boarded
built on contract by migrants

stalking the harvest north
every summer

•

I was born, beauty ended
my appetite for destruction

cock out, tongue fluttering
under the pantry as it emptied

as it emptied, the bottle
of champagne the ground crew gave me

as he descended from the last plane he flew

I remember my father
in the video, mom laughing

as he turns from the ladder

the camera, unsteady
his squadron, their bottles

dousing him too

Nocturne in the gun cabinet   my mother's body in wake
snow falls around me   in the hallways of

THE ARMORY

a bloodhound tracks a dying scent, the snow, white
static, opalescent, sops a half-eaten hare
as I step forward, a chandelier fades.
Night: two doors I walk into
Night Blooming (dear
god Robert)
dear Mother I
walk in
you this
night I
lose
myself
before me
doors I
push
past I
open books
drop, I part them
I come home
Odysseus, beneath
the failing ozone, I part
them, Moses, staff in hand at
the water, the ceiling scattering paint chips
to the corners, somewhere in the wide room a piano
overturned; I turn; my body follows: blackbirds scatter at gunshot
my foot, a ram, like Grendel at the barracks
the air rips my ears—I step through the flung-open doorway to the street

EXIT THEATER

fealty to a tattered flag in steam above the marquee

31

In the gun cabinet
a closet

where I drafted another maker

the hand of M
the drivel

in a Quonset, on a field

a St. Bernard named Hoss chased our church group to a frozen pond

the bridge he slipped from, breaking the ice
the glass I wake under, pricked

blue veil, white dress, red lips

they call my name
they cry it

they lean in & whisper *You first.*

& like the christened, I'm wet
there's blood & water on the walls

the white duvet stripped from the mattress, the floor's half-mandorla, me opposite, curled

like an infant, an insect
sucking a breast

her finger inside me, a circle

then a man comes
white hair

black clothes, black eyes

trumpets

a foghorn he throws me down a palm full of bird's eye a crown full of burl now I've tasted two
    of his frauds

the light sweeps

                through the stained glass

       in vectors
                  through the gun cabinet
    pools of color
        over wood grain

the open cabinet
I wake in

on the mantle, a photograph

my father & I in uniform
(my mother sewed a flight suit

my brothers later wore)

in my hand, wooden biplane
candy red, blue propeller

his hair, my hair
jet black above our smiles

& here now, from my window in the gun cabinet

the trees'

movements in hues of blurred shifting greens in each pixelate square of the window screen—
& I too heavy to sit forward—unlock—lift the glass—each leaf in a barrel roll—

3 or 4 on one axis (each twig & branch—

30, 40 all shimmering, synthesizing, & in flight) & the major branches swinging back & forth

laterally

as if on ecstasy (on the wind, brushing) & me in the chair

like a discharged gun—empty space, window pane, small space, then screen—
the gun cabinet hissing in the background *you heavy sop you*

late you overdue can of beans—

as the leaves fan, frantic, spectral, past the screen; back arched, a girl seething *own*

me through the *tele*—[Gr.]: "far off" (as I am, as she is looking back) *all interspace,*
breath, removal, apotheosis
of my culture—dear bomb, dear discovery of the gaze as determinant of place—dear *definitive state*—

& here at my window, from the top of my window, the trees wave like rescue signals merging in

the gun cabinet, branches hurling upward wrist-deep in the glare

a single leaf lifting itself, a finger (my finger) curls upward, into the space above
& today a white balloon lifts itself all tremolo to the thinned-out blue above the gun cabinet

In the gun cabinet, the bodies you inhabit through your life

                        stand up like guns inside the doors

They open, the flickering present takes you

                  as if by a chain as those bodies form a *V*

                           behind you

    a hand pulls a drawer by a drawer-pull, all

              its lit-up workings applying a lexicon

glittering eyeshadow

            inside the walls, as

    a woman in a white dress

            comes to you in a room

    the curtains drawn

& stage lights beside them

            (*you're searching*

                for something—you don't know)

saying, *In the beginning*

      & she takes down a curtain

           & hands it to you

      heavy & bright

& all of a sudden

        there, in the foreground

      the person you'd become, in relief against shadow

the object you'd searched for

        the word for that

which you had no name

     & by looking, found

a thief

leather gloves

pulled on

you reach in

the drawer

an eye

your hand

a tongue

In the theater
the curtain rises.
It falls, I applaud
& move back a row
through the orchestra, mezzanine
on stage, the same scene
repeats as I lip-sync
the score in each seat.
In the opera, from the nosebleeds
exhausted, I wear
my language trailing
like a bride's train extending
up the stairs I descend
to the last seat I left
with the pair of lorgnettes
I needed at the end
of my vision, a door—no
a veil
at the edge
of experience, a curtain
a garter on the border
of my tale, a vestige
a bride's train climbing
the lip of the stage
an old picture, bleaching
my actor, the way I recall him
my lips part
I pin him, his spine with
my tongue to the frame.
My spit like glass;
his body in motion.
Beneath it, pulsing
a sentence looping
its speaker, a garter, who
wrested, a gun
then turns on herself
suspended

In the gun cabinet, two playgrounds

one for me, one for mother

two men

approach

from the fences.

In the gun cabinet, a hand

his body, my body

inside her, then blackout

in the gun cabinet.

I say *he touched me* [I am acted on]

I say *he grabbed me* [the body acted on]

[they ask me where] I show them [she starts crying]

I say *it hurt* [the act itself]

I say *he hurt me* [his body acted]

I say through acting [his hand] *he hurt me.*

& implicitly I knew it was more than the act

Not *meanness*

Not *violence* (though it felt so) not *thought*

but something else, crushing

fear, transference, that

[in his smile] of which he thought [through me]

he could rid himself

[& his teeth while he did it] [why he only went so far]

& then finding that which he carried

could not [through his own mass] be relieved

finding his hand repeatedly on me *could not*

he withdrew

each time

                    & now, when she speaks to me

I can feel it, the story

her mother never told her (she remembered, then asked)

I can't know (her silence) (which now contains itself) but reason

(from *here*), inescapable fact

of my body

here, inescapable

fact of his & how it acted (he

transposed himself on her) & here

I ask myself if I should (I know I *could*) (despite good reasons) move myself through my idea

of him to forge a dialogue because (reason only goes so far)

the mind requires power not only over others but over its own experience

& so her five brothers & father, after bringing her to my grandmother

after drawing her a bath (not taking her to the hospital) found purpose (asking her

What does he look like How tall What color What did he

speak) in finding him on the other side of the fence near the ravine, at its edge, after asking him

(god knows what) of his mind (his body silent) (as if) (they expected a reason) to answer their questions

they set questions aside & lay their bodies (hands & feet &) the extensions of their bodies into his
     like a cleansing

in the hospitality
of war
We left them their dead
as a gift

—Archilochos

[Cy Twombly, *Epitaph* (1992)– wood, plaster, plywood, & paint, with engraved inscription.
Cy Twombly Gallery, The Menil Collection, Houston.]

When their bodies meet the ground from one hundred & ten stories
ribbons unknotted

so old, they disintegrate (fine red mist) & curl up
into the day

•

into the day, the gun cabinet

you wake

the radio on the table, the airstrike

the first glass of water clean & gleaming

with sunlight

●

in the museums, galleries, archives of a new century

drawers whose mediating walls are rotting, that single image repeating   (I

remember, somewhere, saving the front page because I thought it was worth something)

●

                              above

in that same light

streaming through the dust, the light plays

off your lips as they mime the arc

of the brushstroke's blunt end

We left them their dead as a gift

•

in white paint

to remember us

•

and in the ponds broken off from the sky . . .

•

I

was

delicate

as a child

lived

one too

many lives, I

loved me as myself

I was my brother   last I

entered the gun cabinet   he kept

forgetting who he was, what he wanted, which side

or surface *I* belonged to

•

in his despair, he drew the colors

independent, like letters

from the same word [twenty children

dead &

not even the end of his magazine]

what work to be done   then

•

when the birds falling right out of the sky

the sea mammals blind from the concussions

•

you place the glass down & begin your day

light flecking off the surface, doubled & blinding

on the Formica *rose oh sheer   contradiction*

•

how will I

•

address it   there is a moment from my childhood where my father lifted me

to straddle the 30-millimeter, hydraulically driven, seven-barreled

Gatling cannon

on the nose of the plane he flew

my mother smiled & my younger brother looked up from her shoulders

in awe

there is a picture   I remember

•

what is the value in making now I see   how

will my work speak from its place to this

great violence   *shining*   *white air trembling*   *white light*

                    am I so seduced   I believe

            the time I spend

& what I produce

are untethered to the economy I live by

•

hand that

•

raised   *I*   *reflected*   *the white flat*

sea   look around you

48

•

how you gaze beyond   the gun cabinet

a birth water the better nation does it exist

to an end, our winter

•

what parts of the story were you told *dark evergreen*

what parts

our seaming duration

do you remember   what parts of the story

did you take to be your own

•

Our time here in the gun cabinet is limited

and yet *there, on the other shore*

under the dark gaze of the oak

sun in your eyes   you were there

brother, sister I never knew (here, within my ~~question~~, you

•

you answered)

In the gun cabinet, two chairs (center) face each other. Two cameras on tripods behind them. Between, a small table, a bottle, & two glasses. Lights down over the room, oak paneling & lamplight. I & M seated for an interview.

I: Thank you for joining us. I hope the flight . . .

M: [*fingering a photograph*] It was. [*sets it face-down on the table*] It was . . .

I: I mean, the traffic.

M shrugs.

M: The noise. [*looks up to the ceiling & gestures toward the woodwork*] A strong hand, huh?

I: I believe—

M: [*waving I off*] Wait, wait . . .

They both sit back & look up into the lights.

M: Let's start with fear.

I: Whose fear?

M: Let's talk about *how you talk about* your mother, in the gun cabinet.

I: Shouldn't I—

M: Does it matter?

I: Well, the format . . .

M *shrugs.*

I: It's a problem.

M: A catch.

I: It dictates that I—

M: And I?

I: . . . ask the questions. [*short pause*] Well, I'd like if you—

M: Talk—

I: Well—first, listened—

M: . . . about your mother, who at best, is held outward: a door. Then the Madonna, a small moment of pornography—

I: Our relationship *necessitates*—

M: Our—hour.

Brief pause.

M: The father. [*pointing at* I] *There's* a figure. And the brother . . .

I: *And* Mother.

M: *And* Mother.

They pause as M *lights a cigarette.*

M: It's not that she's passive. She's [*exhales*] *clipped.*

I: Cheated.

M: Like hair.

I: As scissors do.

M: Now you're getting it. Imagine a pet store. [*tosses the pack toward the table*] So the birds can't—

It lands with a thud.

I: But it's not—

M: You can muster it.

I pauses.

I: You mean *gather.*

M: Collect.

I: *Mother.*

M: Macaw—from the Latin *monstrare.* To show.

I: To *show* . . .

M: A bird . . . *on display?*

I: Who's conducting this!?

M: Hooo!

I: We need clarity.

M: Should I leave?

M stands & looks to the exit. I touches M's arm.

I: No. [*quietly*] Please—

I gestures toward the open seat. M stops, one hand on I's backrest, then returns to the chair.

I: Let's start elsewhere.

M: An exit.

I shrugs.

M: How convenient.

They pause. Then, eyes locked:

M: One more question.

I: Then you're through?

M nods.

I: All you.

M flicks the end of the cigarette out onto the stage & sits forward, extending a hand as if holding a microphone or offering an open palm.

M: I, who mothered whom?

I nods.

I: That's true.

M: [*smiling, aside*] Is there wine?

THIRD PERSON (offstage):   Is there!

A THIRD PERSON, dressed in black, white waiters cloth over one arm, enters stage left, pours wine from the bottle, & exits. They drink.

M: You had a question?

I: [*tipping the glass back*] Mm. [*swallows*] Did I?

M: I believe . . .

I: [*lowering the glass*] Wait, wait . . .

I places the glass on the table, takes a cigarette, and, pausing, considers it.

M: I thought you'd given it up.

I: Well it's hard, these days.

M: You mean the traffic.

I shrugs.

I: The noise.

I lights it. A brief pause. They both look up into the lights.

I: [*exhales, raising the cigarette to eye level*] It's a funny thing, you know. But you're right. [*puts the cigarette out on shoe, then tosses the butt on the table*]

They pause.

I: I was wishing.

M: Wishing.

I leans forward, toward M. M takes the butt, sits back & crosses legs.

I: I was wishing I could be more like you.

M lights it.

M: I am making you like me. [*flicks the butt out onto the stage*]

I: Oh, M. [*shakes head, sitting back in the chair*] I keep forgetting.

M: Oh, I. [*strikes a match & lights a new one*] I'm sorry.

EXIT THEATER

Song / Little Myth (Catullus 65)

That unremitting siphon, grief, tears me from my desk.

                   Exhausted mind, dead tree, no apple at my lips. Friend, I try—
my every thought the water's tongue, his white foot.

                   Know this: beauty concealed, our loved ones pulled from view.
The shore of a state carves the dirt of a city it felled by trickery

                       in war—my line erased—brother, I loved you more
than the eye I bear toward an end that keeps you from it. That love

                   a constant garment absence wears in the outline of a voice.
I sing into the suck of it. And the swallow, thrumming

                   sings with me in the shadow of a branch in the voice of the child
she fed—her own—to her husband. That's what I mean

                   by silence, the female nightingale mute. So she makes
the swallow sing the crime: *Her man, his hand, my mouth.*

                   Agony aside, friend, here are the poems you asked for.
Once, a girl was promised love by a boy who meant to keep it.

                   The promise took the form of an apple, the boy the form
of dirt. When he left (the war) she stayed, the apple

                   in her lap, until she stood in a gust of wind and it ran
the crease of her dress. She looked down: tall grass.

                   I suppose she never found it. Imagine her plump cheeks
drained of blush, but for the gathering dark. And my face?

                   I keep my word. Here are the poems you asked for.

noun. a polyp
of solipsism

irrefutable by its own postulate

indefensible, too
a hostile nation

a citizen of

engaging in

activities against

foe, opponent, adversary
antagonist, a list

of faces one might hide or highlight

finger, frame
oppose with force

a joining, pointing
match

As Her Myriad Aggressors
(Poem Returning to a Line Spoken by Ophelia)

OPHELIA: *You are naught, you are naught: I'll mark the play.*

POLONIUS: *I'll teach you*
think yourself

baby / be
scanter

•

POLONIUS: *Running it thus / daughter*
POLONIUS / HAMLET: *you'll tender me / God*

has given you one face
and you make / another.

•

MICHAEL: That a body be   wail.

vessel, harpoon
and what's

left when hunted
bade blue and through.

•

OPHELIA: *Hey*
                       nonny

                       non nonny
                       hey, nonny / hey.

                       You are naught, you are naught: I'll mark the play.

As His Myriad Objections
(Poem Returning to a Line Spoken by Brutus)

BRUTUS: *Slaying is the word. It is a deed in fashion.*

CLITUS: *What ill request?*
DARDANIUS: *To kill . . .*

Look—

•

MICHAEL: That language be   fails.

the cart by which
our resistance

and profit
meet, and wage.

•

MICHAEL: I paid good money for my language.

Good time, too.
Killed time spent

drafting beast
burden, and sale.

•

CAESAR: *And you—*

What touches us
ourself, shall be last served.

BRUTUS: *Slaying is the word. It is a deed—*

Twenty-Four Exits (A Closet Drama)

A theater. White noise from the speakers, white light
under the curtains. They part to reveal a large, brightly lit screen.

[applause]

MALE VOICE (center): I know my entire state
is looking forward to heat . . . *[tape cut]*

       heat without humanity

[tape scrub] . . . heat without humidity

[applause]

heat by steam production
commensurate with fuel-rod insertion

kept from our neighbors to the east.

[wild applause]

MALE VOICE (left): Things happen . . . *unnaturally.*

MALE VOICE (right): Traffic's always . . . *[static]*.

"Like a hot knife to butter," the ENGINEER chirps.
[enters stage left, thumbs through a file]

"Motorcycles overheat. Gasses leak. Uranium's a mysterious business." [HE *exits*]

The reel begins, the audience shifts.

PICTURE START

8   7   6   5   4   3   [*beep*]

[*pompous music*]

On-screen: A montage. Bodies in lab coats. Flags & brass bands.

ENGINEER'S VOICE (stage left, in an echo): Majid Shahriari, Ardeshir
Hosseinpour, Masoud Alimohammadi, Darioush Rezaeinejad.

Wiping her brow at the heart of intelligence
the SECRETARY's *knuckles in blue.*

[*cut*]

Dust blowing. Cracked dirt and shrubs.
An envelope changes hands.

[*music out*]

THE MOSSAD: Go.

STUXNET: Going.

CENTRIFUGE: Whatever you say.

[*wild applause*]

The aisles light up. The screen goes white.

INTERMISSION

The aisle lights flash. The audience settles.
The screen fades on, white, over one chair.

PICTURE START

8   7   6   5   4   3   *[beep]*

On-screen: Int. Diner and gas station.

[MAN *in glasses & white taqiyah*
enters stage left, moves center toward the chair]

MAN (sitting): Put this in your underwear.

Three men at a table, eating.

FEMALE VOICE (right): This is JSOC to flight control.

MAN: Belligerents
who also happen

to be

US citizens
do not enjoy

immunity where
noncitizen belligerents

are valid military objectives.

67

On-screen: Ext. A dirt road. A Jeep weaving.
Hills and roving crosshairs.

MALE VOICE (right): Saba reports . . .

FEMALE VOICE (left): . . . al-Awlaki killed.

MALE VOICE (right): Two weeks later, at a cookout . . .

FEMALE VOICE (left): . . . his 16-year-old son.

The screen pans out to frame another. A sharp tilt, then, an explosion.

FEMALE VOICE (right): Fox 2. Splash.

FEMALE VOICE (left): Fox News reports . . .

MALE VOICE (right): Abdul-Rahman . . .

FEMALE VOICE (left): . . . his 21-year-old son.

[*pause, then applause, building up to a crescendo*]

MALE VOICE (right): Saba—

[MAN *exits*]

FEMALE VOICE (left): . . . a number of his fellow [*static*]—[*applause*]. Samir Khan, a
US citizen . . .

MALE VOICE (right): . . . to *Inspire* magazine:

MALE VOICE 2 (offstage, un-mic'd): I am proud to be a traitor to America . . .

[*curtains*]

. . . If you give Satan an inch, he'll be a ruler.

If Nothing Else, Pleasure (Catullus 76)

If nothing else, pleasure
That even though others die
it is not by my hands themselves. Now
& has not broken fraternity, or bone
deceived a neighbor by hand or spectacle
joy remain?
And if no one really hears
& every eye nooseward
& it heralds a commons
& at whom?
Don't take it as an end.
You know it's hard to cast off love, to lead yourself back
Find a way.
up the steps, to the temple
Laugh in the face of the guard & spit
Look in its stone eye, say what it knows
I'm here to wash your feet for a price.
What wretch, ever spared. What dog. What girl.
I am clean.
My throat, its veins.
A voice I never asked to speak in
One thing. Reprieve.
I know what it is

just knowing one's own borders.
because of my hands' extensions
if one believes in a private kindness
nor through any deal with awe
does not, if nothing else
Let it continue through my life.
through the news of the day, tinged in green
if my tongue simply gestures
what stone should be cast
Good intentions fade. That's a crisis.
Wade through it.
to pleasure.
Carry its open corpse like a purse
& drop it.
on the gold-plated feet of the statue.
it was fashioned, a likeness, to hear.
Look at me. Lord, what grace.
And me.
Touch my white skin.
I think of nothing else.
booms in my bluest cavity.
Pleasure. Please.
is happening.

The world is not far off from here. Not far off . . .

•

Have you ever (in solitude) spoken in the voice of a stranger?

I read a story in the news today. My voice, Calvin Gibbs. My voice ballistic in the living room.

•

This is

close to me. I repeat as I work overlooking the park, windows shut against the wind.

•

The world is not far off. Not far . . .

With my instruction, this monologue begins.

•

Hold a boy and a pitcher at the edge of your mind and listen.

•

A woman steps out onto a porch, *country summer.* Rear shot, *the view from her legs down, the bricks under her feet.*

Not *the scuttle of leaves* unfallen, not *the black seams of her stockings* running the backs of her legs. Nothing of her shoes. She is barefoot. A simple housedress wraps her legs in the wind.

•

Place the pitcher on a stoop and walk inside. Dread the doorbell, the neighbors' reckless children.

•

Here, Calvin. In your finity of confusion, of frustration, hell in the task you were set to.

On the one side, their pleading, then the wall. Then the other side with you and the field.

•

The world, Calvin, *is not far.*

•

Let me explain. We have to start here, confusing the characters, switching the costumes, forgetting the lines.

Start with dragging the trunk out into the common room.

●

I said *monologue*. I meant *dialogue*.

For these few hours before night falls, *talk*. There cannot be another day.

●

Out of a suffering made present, that which you shared.

Out of this matter, which defies matter, a weight between things.

●

From this place I drag out your story.

●

OLD TAPE: [. . . *indecipherable*] *feet-first out of a pit by his friends*

whose boots kick dust into his face like an open fruit.

●

Out of a world of confusion, frustration I know had source. Out of that within you which knew.

A voice knowing only itself.

•

Can I explain? You put bags of tea into water.

You bring them out to the sun.

•

The world, Calvin.

Not far.

•

OLD TAPE: [. . .] *on a stretcher in the back of a C-17.*

Here's Frankfurt. Here's Bolling. This is where his hearing returns.

•

To the woman I say, *This is your child*, and I hand her a piece of fruit.

To another I say, *This is your husband.* I see you leading him to a field and asking him to kneel.

•

Out of a war created, like milk from a stone.

Out of recalcitrance(?), boredom(?), you asked two men to watch.

●

The explosion, they said, *"tore the man apart."*

●

Out of this suffering made *unjust I know* for you to enter, I imagine a room like a vault.

And through ~~language, speaking,~~ *dialogue*(??) the code, breaking like "accidental discharge" on the other side of a wall.

●

CONTEMPORARY RECORDING (calmly, with measure): [. . .] *words that bark off into rotor wash like dogs into country night. Moths. A fold of purple ribbon, a piece of metal to mirror the hole cut out for his nose.*

●

At the end of a hallway, down a red length of carpet, I come to a white door, ajar. No light reaches past. Smell of must like an old hotel, screw holes where the numbers were removed.

Into that room I put my hand.

●

What I pull out startles me. First a truck, then another, then another—a string. An entire convoy, suspended,

moving toward a huddle of tents.

You walk up to me from behind and hand me a canvas bag. I take the bag and place my hand inside it.

CONTEMPORARY RECORDING: [. . .] *He takes off his uniform, drapes it in plastic, and opens his closet.*

One grenade.

Two molars.

One piece of skull.

Three fingers, from the second knuckle down.

Off the books, you say. The hallway walls and the carpet disappear.

You turn into the space that opens before us, climbing into the back of a truck.

A door. The paint (worn down). The wood (exposed).

One lamp reaches down from above.

●

I turn around and think: *interrogation.* Where the door was, a heap of woodchips.

●

I take the grenade from the bag, pull the pin, wait. When the trucks stop firing, I hold the bag up with my thumb and forefinger, inside out.

I let it hang there, holes everywhere.

●

OLD TAPE: [. . . *loud scrubbing, then silence. Classical music and radio broadcasts from previous recordings*] . . . some of them on their fourth . . . [*static*].

★   ★   ★

I'm sitting down now to tea with you.

●

See, that's you at the center of a long table, the door we both know, on its back. On either side of you, your men sit, eating. I stand on the other side of the table, the one lamp hanging above. The light thins out a few yards beyond us. Behind you, barely visible, a man in a wheelchair whom no one else sees.

●

CONTEMPORARY RECORDING (slower, with a drop in tone): *Every morning, mother drives him to the clinic.*

●

I start to ask you a question.

I sit.

●

CONTEMPORARY RECORDING (holding the low note): *There's a flat screen in the corner that always plays the news.*

●

One by one, all around us, forming a perimeter in the dark, images of our decade blink on and play at random. Simulations, computer games, mass graves—wedding cakes and narrow passages in black and white—tracer bullets and flak lighting up a green sky.

Your men look up from their mess trays and turn around in their seats.

●

OLD TAPE: [*crackling, indecipherable noises . . .*]

[*light beside light beside light beside light . . .*]

●

At the end of our table, there is a woman, looking away.

She turns to face us.

●

OLD TAPE: [*sound of spooling . . .*] ***Let night fall.***

●

Everyone hears a click.

•

Darkness takes us, and I hear you say *candies along the road* . . .

A last screen flickers, and I hear the one man rolling back out of range.

•

Somewhere in this story, there is a dress that will never be worn again. *Cue housedress hanging from the rafters over the porch.*

Somewhere, the shot out onto the lawn.

•

Elsewhere, a young farmer approaches two soldiers.

•

But where we are now, it's just you and me. No light. No sound. Just this surface beneath our elbows, a photograph we can't see, lying flat on the table.

•

Calvin,

You gave us an image. A likeness of ourselves.

●

OLD TAPE: [*skips, then a brief vocal sound*]

●

Here. I've come to you

to ask you our story.

●

Put your hands on the table. Put your hands in mine.

●

Do you understand? Now I can't tell us

apart.

●

MICHAEL: *The world is not* [. . .]

●

Now I can't tell where I end.

Notes & Acknowledgements

This book would not be what it is without Tyrone Williams, who selected it for the 2016 Colorado Prize for Poetry, and Stephanie G'Schwind, the Director of the Center for Literary Publishing at Colorado State University. Thank you.

The Catullus poems were written using online sources and via other English translations. Google Translate filled in the gaps. I am indebted to Grace Andreacci, Aubrey Beardsley, Anne Carson, Peter Green, A. S. Kline, Rudy Negenborn, James Peters, Brendan Rau, and H. J. Walker.

"Say Goodbye to the Shores (Catullus 101)" takes its title from *Say Goodbye Catullus, to the Shores of Asia Minor* (Cy Twombly. 1994), on permanent display at the Cy Twombly Gallery, the Menil Collection, Houston.

"Lydia" was written in response to the Metropolitan Museum of Art's 2013 exhibition *Matisse: In Search of True Painting,* and debuted at a reading at the Met organized by Rachel Zucker and Katherine Nemeth in March 2013.

"The Wall that Consumes All before It (Reverse Ilium)" takes its refrain from the 1978 Cy Twombly painting *Fifty Days at Iliam (The Fire that Consumes All before It),* on permanent display at the Philadelphia Art Museum. The poem references a dance by Jonah Bokaer, *On Vanishing,* performed in 2011 on the ground floor of the Guggenheim New York, during Lee Ufan's retrospective, *Marking Infinity.*

"Portraits of the Artists as Their Own Subjects" is indebted to Jonathan Rajewski, Catherine Lepp, Matthew Zingg, Pina Bausch, Dylan Rogers, Anne Marie O'Neill, Sarah Michelson, Zachary Nichols, Brandon Lake, Sharon Kirby, and Carla Edwards.

The second section of "In the Gun Cabinet," [there's a violence], uses language from Guns N' Roses' debut studio album, *Appetite for Destruction* (Geffen, 1987), as well as Jorie Graham's *The End of Beauty* (Ecco, 1987).

The final section of "In the Gun Cabinet," [in the hospitality of war], uses language (in italics) from a number of Cy Twombly paintings and sculptures, including *Epitaph* (1992); *Untitled, a Painting in 9 Parts* (1988); *Analysis of the Rose as Sentimental Despair* (1985); and *Say Goodbye Catullus, to the Shores of Asia Minor* (1994), which quote from Archilochus, Rilke, Rumi, Catullus, and George Seferis, with additions (and changes) by Twombly himself. All are on permanent display at the Cy Twombly Gallery, the Menil Collection, Houston. A special thank you to Delana Bunch at the Menil for her help.

"As Her Myriad Aggressors (Poem Returning to a Line Spoken by Ophelia)" and "As His Myriad Objections (Poem Returning to a Line Spoken by Brutus)" take italicized text from quotes spoken by Ophelia and her aggressors in Shakespeare's *Hamlet*, and by Caesar and his assassins in *Julius Caesar*, respectively. Forward slashes indicate a splicing of the speech in the plays.

"Twenty-Four Exits (A Closet Drama)" takes quotes from *Saturday Night Live*, Season 1: Episode 1, "The Impossible Truth" (Headline: Israel and Georgia Trade Places); Israeli Army Lt. General Benny Gantz; Mostafa Ahmadi-Roshan; the *New York Times* article "Iran Reports Killing of Nuclear Scientist in 'Terrorist' Blast" (1/11/12); the *New York Times Magazine* feature "Will Israel Attack Iran?" (1/25/12); the *New York Times* article "Obama Order Sped Up Wave of Cyberattacks Against Iran" (6/1/12); the *New York Times* visual feature "How a Secret Cyberwar Program Worked" (6/1/12); the *Huffington Post* article "Antiwar Movement Successfully Pushes Back Against Military Confrontation with Iran" (7/31/08); the *Washington Post* article "A 'proud traitor': Samir Khan reported dead alongside Aulaqi [sic]" (9/30/11); Jeh Johnson (Pentagon General Counsel, Feb. 2012, public record); Saba article "US-most wanted Al-Awlaki killed in Yemen airstrike" (9/30/11); Fox News/Associated Press article "Al-Awlaki's Son Among Al Qaeda Militants Killed in Yemen Air Strike" (10/15/11); *Inspire* issue II, fall 2010 interview with Samir Khan (as reported by the *Washington Post*); and from Samir Khan's 2003 yearbook quote (as reported by the *Washington Post*).

"Self_Interrogation (Kill Team)" responds to true events researched through *Der Spiegel, Rolling Stone,* the *Washington Post,* and others. I am unable to find the original *WaPo* article.

Thank you to the editors & staff at the following publications, where many of these poems first appeared: *Artifice;* the *Awl; Boston Review;* the *Brooklyn Rail; Colorado Review; Denver Quarterly; Diagram; Everyday Genius; Fence; Jubilat; La Petite Zine;* the *Mackinac; No, Dear; OmniVerse; Pank; Paperbag;* the PEN *Poetry Series; Prelude;* and *Volt.*

Thanks to Elizabeth Devlin for including several poems in The Highwaymen NYC chapbooks, and in the 2013 Anthology.

Parts of "In the Gun Cabinet" were printed in *Symbolic Castration,* a public arts installation/publication in Eastern Market, Detroit, and as part of an installation at Burnside Farm, Detroit. Thanks to Jonathan Rajewski and Kate Daughdrill.

"Exit Theater (A Closet Drama)" was included in the *Papercut Annual 2013* and in the *Albion Beatnik,* published by the Albion Beanik Bookstore, Oxford, United Kingdom. Thanks to Sarah Lerner and Maggie Craig, and Dennis Harris and Dan Holloway.

"Exit Theater (A Closet Drama)" was subsequently published by Danny Snelson and Mashinka Firunts as a Present Tense Pamphlet, in conjunction with the *Performed in the Present Tense* symposium and *A Feast of Astonishments: Charlotte Moorman and the Avant-Garde, 1960s–1980s* exhibition at the Mary & Leigh Block Museum of Art at Northwestern University, Evanston, Illinois, 2016.

"In the Gun Cabinet" was published as a chapbook by the *Atlas Review* as part of the TAR Chapbook Series in February 2016. A huge, heartfelt thank you to Natalie Eilbert, Emily Raw, Dolan Morgan, Tom Oristaglio, Jeremy Michael Clark, Lynley Shimat Lys, Jayson Smith, Amy Brinker, and everyone at the *Atlas Review.*

Thank you to Zachary Nichols and Miki Yamada Foster for designing sound for the performance of various parts of *Exit Theater.* Thank you to Harry Bertoia.

Thank you, finally, to Allyson Paty, Jonathan Rajewski, Yusef Komunyakaa, Cathy Linh Che, Alaina Ferris, Natalie Eilbert, Anne Carson, Stanley Lombardo, CL Young, Ruth Greenstein, Meghan O'Rourke, Robin Coste Lewis, Marina Weiss, Eric Nelson, Deborah Landau, Emily Barton Altman, Toby Altman, Anna Moschovakis, Sharon Olds, Rachel Zucker, Craig Morgan Teicher, Matthew Rohrer, and Diane Wakoski for their eyes, suggestions, and support.

This book is set in Sabon
by The Center for Literary Publishing
at Colorado State University.

Copyediting by CL Young.
Proofreading by Sam Killmeyer.
Book design and typesetting by Meghan Pipe.
Cover design by Stephanie G'Schwind.
Printing by BookMobile.